Paul and Thecla

The Church

and the Strong Willed Woman

Joseph Lumpkin

Paul and Thecla
The Church and the Strong Willed Woman
Copyright © 2015 Joseph Lumpkin
All rights reserved.
Printed in the United States of America. No part of
this book may be used or reproduced in any
manner whatsoever without written permission
except in the case of brief quotations embodied in
critical articles and reviews.

Fifth Estate Publishers
Blountsville, AL 35031.

First edition 2015
Cover art by An Quigley
Printed on acid-free paper

Library of Congress Control No: 2015904773
ISBN: 9781936533510

Fifth Estate

Paul and Thecla: The Church and the Strong Willed Woman

Joseph Lumpkin

Table of Contents

Preface

The Acts of Paul and Thecla was written around 150 CE when there was a growing body of work attributed to the apostle Paul. Owing to the abrupt beginning of the work it is thought The Acts of Paul and Thecla was part of a larger texts and was extracted to form a stand alone work. Reasons given for its omission from the Bible are numerous. It was thought to have been written after the apostolic age. It gives high and powerful position to women in the faith. It urges women to withhold sex from their husbands and live chaste lives.

Within its storyline Thecla seems to eclipse Paul in her courage and commitment to the spread of the Gospel. The text presents an unwavering stance on the virtue of celibacy preached by Paul and amplified by Thecla. In addition, Thecla is presented as a strong willed woman who took it upon herself to preach, teach, heal, and baptize, all without permission or oversight from a man.

In the age when canon was being decided, women in positions of leadership within the church was an anomaly, and the idea that a wife could decide her own fate, and even withhold sex from her husband was looked upon as heresy and insolence. These were social constraints, which tainted the interpretation of scripture, both then and now.

We will examine the true place of women in the Bible and how translators diminished the place and accomplishments of women by mistranslating words and phrases. We will look at the true meaning of many Bible verses as well as the complete text of Paul and Thecla, with an eye toward how women were a driving force in religion and family in the early church. In the end, a more true and just vision of women of the Bible and of ancient times will be revealed.

Joseph Lumpkin

The Bible and the Feminine Types

The nature and position of women are exemplified in the personages of Deborah, Abigail, Priscilla, Eunice, Phoebe, and others, whose names have been omitted from the Bible because they were simply too strong. Most women, whose stories we find in the Bible, fall into two types. They are determined, devoted, demure, and acted with decorum. or they are wayward, wanton, and wicked. There is a also a noticeable shift in the permitted positions of women between the Old Testament and New Testament.

In the Old Testament, we are more likely to find a more complete picture of the female psyche than we find in the New Testament. Socially, the view of women becomes even more simplistic in the post New Testament world. To see a panoramic view a picture must be painted with a composite made up of several women. There are women who are like those who Solomon's mother sees as the perfect

9

wife and wishes Solomon to seek out. There are those who are simply wiser than their husbands, but who work behind the scenes to correct his mistakes. Then, there are those who are warriors and prophets.

We will look quickly at these three divergent types. They are the positive attributes as presented in the Old Testament. They are the faces of the Sacred Feminine exemplified in the pages of the Bible.

The ideal and perfect woman at the time of Solomon, is summed up in Proverbs 31. She provided tireless support and devotion to her family. She was above reproach. She is the archetype of Mother Mary in the Jungian schema.

Proverbs 31:10-31
(Message Bible)
A good woman is hard to find, and worth far more than diamonds.
Her husband trusts her without reserve,
  and never has reason to regret it.

Never spiteful, she treats him generously
  all her life long.
She shops around for the best yarns and cottons,
  and enjoys knitting and sewing.
She's like a trading ship that sails to faraway places and
brings back exotic surprises.
She's up before dawn, preparing breakfast
  for her family and organizing her day.
She looks over a field and buys it,
  then, with money she's put aside, plants a garden.
First thing in the morning, she dresses for work,
  rolls up her sleeves, eager to get started.
She senses the worth of her work,
  is in no hurry to call it quits for the day.
She's skilled in the crafts of home and hearth,
  diligent in homemaking.
She's quick to assist anyone in need,
  reaches out to help the poor.
She doesn't worry about her family when it snows; their
winter clothes are all mended and ready to wear.
She makes her own clothing,
  and dresses in colorful linens and silks.

Her husband is greatly respected

  when he deliberates with the city fathers.

She designs gowns and sells them,

  brings the sweaters she knits to the dress shops.

Her clothes are well-made and elegant,

  and she always faces tomorrow with a smile.

When she speaks she has something worthwhile to say,

 and she always says it kindly.

She keeps an eye on everyone in her household,

  and keeps them all busy and productive.

Her children respect and bless her;

  her husband joins in with words of praise:

"Many women have done wonderful things,

  but you've outclassed them all!"

Charm can mislead and beauty soon fades.

  The woman to be admired and praised

  is the woman who lives in the Fear-of-God.

Give her everything she deserves!

  Festoon her life with praises!

We also see women who were wiser than there male counterparts, and act independently of them in order to save both themselves and their foolish husbands. The women may have defied their husbands but they repaired and balanced the situation. Owning to the Gnostic belief that Mary Magdalene was given special knowledge over and above the other disciples, we will call this woman the "Mary Magdalene" of the Jungian types.

Abigail
1 Samuel 25
(Message Bible)

1) Samuel died. The whole country came to his funeral. Everyone grieved over his death, and he was buried in his hometown of Ramah. Meanwhile, David moved again, this time to the wilderness of Maon.

2-3) There was a certain man in Maon who carried on his business in the region of Carmel. He was very prosperous – three thousand sheep and a thousand goats, and it was sheep-shearing time in Carmel. The man's name was Nabal (Fool), a Calebite, and his wife's name was Abigail. The woman was intelligent and good-looking, the man brutish and mean.

4-8) David, out in the backcountry, heard that Nabal was shearing his sheep and sent ten of his young men off with these instructions: "Go to Carmel and approach Nabal. Greet him in my name, 'Peace! Life and peace to you. Peace to your household, peace to everyone here! I heard that it's sheep-shearing time. Here's the point: When your shepherds were camped near us, we didn't take advantage of them. They didn't lose a thing all the time they were with us in Carmel. Ask your young men – they'll tell you. What I'm asking is that you be generous with my men – share the feast! Give whatever your heart tells you to your servants and to me, David your son."

9-11) David's young men went and delivered his message word for word to Nabal. Nabal tore into them, "Who is this David? Who is this son of Jesse? The country is full of runaway servants these days. Do you think I'm going to take good bread and wine and meat freshly butchered for my sheepshearers and give it to men I've never laid eyes on? Who knows where they've come from?"

12-13) David's men got out of there and went back and told David what he had said. David said, "Strap on your swords!" They all strapped on their swords, David and his men, and set out, four hundred of them. Two hundred stayed behind to guard the camp.

14-17) Meanwhile, one of the young shepherds told Abigail, Nabal's wife, what had happened: "David sent messengers from the backcountry to salute our master, but he tore into them with insults. Yet these men treated us very well. They took nothing from us and didn't take advantage of us all the time we were in the fields. They formed a wall around us, protecting us day and night all the time we were out tending the sheep. Do something quickly because big trouble is ahead for our master and all of us. Nobody can talk to him. He's impossible – a real brute!"

18-19) Abigail flew into action. She took two hundred loaves of bread, two skins of wine, five sheep dressed out and ready for cooking, a bushel of roasted grain, a hundred raisin cakes, and two hundred fig cakes, and she had it all loaded on some donkeys. Then she said to her young servants, "Go ahead and pave the way for me. I'm right behind you." But she said nothing to her husband Nabal.

20-22) *As she was riding her donkey, descending into a ravine, David and his men were descending from the other end, so they met there on the road. David had just said, "That sure was a waste, guarding everything this man had out in the wild so that nothing he had was lost — and now he rewards me with insults. A real slap in the face! May God do his worst to me if Nabal and every cur in his misbegotten brood aren't dead meat by morning!"*

23-25) *As soon as Abigail saw David, she got off her donkey and fell on her knees at his feet, her face to the ground in homage, saying, "My master, let me take the blame! Let me speak to you. Listen to what I have to say. Don't dwell on what that brute Nabal did. He acts out the meaning of his name: Nabal, Fool. Foolishness oozes from him."*

25-27) *I wasn't there when the young men my master sent arrived. I didn't see them. And now, my master, as God lives and as you live, God has kept you from this avenging murder — and may your enemies, all who seek my master's harm, end up like Nabal! Now take this gift that I, your servant girl, have brought to my master, and give it to the young men who follow in the steps of my master.*

28-29) "Forgive my presumption! But God is at work in my master, developing a rule solid and dependable. My master fights God's battles! As long as you live no evil will stick to you. If anyone stands in your way, if anyone tries to get you out of the way, know this: Your God-honored life is tightly bound in the bundle of God-protected life; but the lives of your enemies will be hurled aside as a stone is thrown from a sling.

30-31) "When God completes all the goodness he has promised my master and sets you up as prince over Israel, my master will not have this dead weight in his heart, the guilt of an avenging murder. And when God has worked things for good for my master, remember me."

32-34) And David said, "Blessed be God, the God of Israel. He sent you to meet me! And blessed be your good sense! Bless you for keeping me from murder and taking charge of looking out for me. A close call! As God lives, the God of Israel who kept me from hurting you, if you had not come as quickly as you did, stopping me in my tracks, by morning there would have been

17

nothing left of Nabal but dead meat."

35) Then David accepted the gift she brought him and said, "Return home in peace. I've heard what you've said and I'll do what you've asked."

36-38) When Abigail got home she found Nabal presiding over a huge banquet. He was in high spirits — and very, very drunk. So she didn't tell him anything of what she'd done until morning. But in the morning, after Nabal had sobered up, she told him the whole story. Right then and there he had a heart attack and fell into a coma. About ten days later God finished him off and he died.

39-40) When David heard that Nabal was dead he said, "Blessed be God who has stood up for me against Nabal's insults, kept me from an evil act, and let Nabal's evil boomerang back on him."

Then David sent for Abigail to tell her that he wanted her for his wife. David's servants went to Abigail at Carmel with the message, "David sent us to bring you to marry him."

There is little doubt that the story below exemplifies "Sophia" in the Jungian types.

Joseph Lumpkin

Deborah was a prophet and judge over Israel who sensed the timing of God. She was fearless, independent, and wise.

Jael was a woman who defied the ill begotten alliance between her husband, Heber, and the evil king, Jabin. Jael killed Sisera by driving a tent peg through his head and into the ground.

Deborah

Judges 2

18 And when the Lord raised them up judges, then the Lord was with the judge, and delivered them out of the hand of their enemies all the days of the judge: for it repented the Lord because of their groanings by reason of them that oppressed them and vexed them.

Judges 4

(Message Bible)

1-3) The people of Israel kept right on doing evil in God's sight. With Ehud dead, God sold them off to Jabin, king of Canaan, who ruled from Hazor. Sisera, who lived in Harosheth Haggoyim, was the commander of his army. The people of Israel cried out to God because he had cruelly oppressed them with his nine hundred iron chariots for twenty years.

4-5) Deborah was a prophet, the wife of Lappidoth. She was judge over Israel at that time. She held court under Deborah's Palm between Ramah and Bethel in the hills of Ephraim. The People of Israel went to her in matters of justice.

6-7) She sent for Barak, son of Abinoam from Kedesh in Naphtali, and said to him, "It has become clear that God, the God of Israel, commands you: 'Go to Mount Tabor and prepare for battle. Take ten companies of soldiers from Naphtali and Zebulun. I'll take care of getting Sisera, the leader of Jabin's army, to the Kishon River with all his chariots and troops. And I'll make sure you win the battle'."

8) Barak said, "If you go with me, I'll go. But if you don't go with me, I won't go."

9-10) * She said, "Of course I'll go with you. But understand that with an attitude like that, there'll be no glory in it for you. *

God will use a woman's hand to take care of Sisera."

(Note: The words between the * are not in the Septuagint.)

Deborah got ready and went with Barak to Kedesh.   Barak called Zebulun and Naphtali together at Kedesh.   Ten companies of men followed him. And Deborah was with him.

11-13) It happened that Heber, the Kenite, had parted company with the other Kenites, the descendants of Hobab, Moses' in-law. He was now living at Zaanannim Oak near Kedesh. They told Sisera that Barak, son of Abinoam, had gone up to Mount Tabor. Sisera immediately called up all his chariots to the Kishon River—nine hundred iron chariots!—along with all his troops who were with him at Harosheth Haggoyim.

14) Deborah said to Barak, "Charge! This very day God has given you victory over Sisera. Isn't God marching before you?"

Barak charged down the slopes of Mount Tabor, his ten companies following him.

15-16) God routed Sisera—all those chariots, all

those troops! — before Barak.   Sisera jumped out of his chariot and ran. Barak chased the chariots and troops all the way to Harosheth Haggoyim. Sisera's entire fighting force was killed — not one man left.

17-18) Meanwhile Sisera, running for his life, headed for the tent of Jael, wife of Heber, the Kenite.   Jabin, king of Hazor, and Heber, the Kenite, were on good terms with one another. Jael stepped out to meet Sisera and said, "Come in, sir. Stay here with me. Don't be afraid."

So he went with her into her tent. She covered him with a blanket.

19) He said to her, "Please, a little water. I'm thirsty."

She opened a bottle of milk, gave him a drink, and then covered him up again.

20) He then said, "Stand at the tent flap. If anyone comes by and asks you, 'Is there anyone here? 'tell him, 'No, not a soul.'"

21) Then, while he was fast asleep from exhaustion, Jael, wife of Heber, took a tent peg and hammer, tiptoed toward him, and drove the tent peg through his temple and all the way into the

ground. He convulsed and died.

22) Barak arrived in pursuit of Sisera. Jael went out to greet him. She said, "Come, I'll show you the man you're looking for." He went with her and there he was—Sisera, stretched out, dead, with a tent peg through his temple.

23-24) On that day, God subdued Jabin, king of Canaan, before the people of Israel. The people of Israel pressed harder and harder on Jabin king of Canaan until there was nothing left of him.

In Judges 2:18, we are told God raised up judges, rulers, and leaders for the nation of Israel. This was to deliver them from the surrounding heathen nations. We are also told that God raised up the judges and God was with the judges. In Judges Chapter 4, God has chosen Deborah as judge and prophet.

Deborah calls for Barak, a mighty warrior to gather 10,000 men from the tribes of Nephthali and Zebulon. It is God's time to deliver His people from the oppression of the heathen king of Canaan. Barak presents himself before Judge Deborah and is given the strategy for victory.

An expansion of verse 8, found only in the Septuagint, places everything in perspective.

In verse 8 of Judges 4, Barak says to Deborah:
"I will go if you will go with me, and if you will not go, I will not go, for I know not the day the Lord prospers His messenger with me."

Barak is saying to Deborah, you have the timing of the Lord for this battle. There were no cell phones, radios etc. Barak needed the prophet to know when to strike the death blow to Jabin's army and Jabin's military leader, Sisera.

He was NOT a wimp. He was not hiding behind a woman. He was strong and brave; a man who led and commanded 10,000 warriors.

Even when Deborah told Barak that, a woman,

Jael, would get the glory for killing Sisera, he did not flinch. What a man of character and valor. So the God plan begins. Deborah, Barak, and 10,000 mighty men camped at the river Kison.

Barak knew that Deborah had the timing of God for the battle. Deborah calls out, "Get up!!! Today is the day!" And so it was.

Sisera and the 900 chariots of iron and all the soldiers of Canaan were overthrown. Sisera fled on foot to the tent of Heber, who had a pact with Jabin to lodge or help the Canaanites who came his way. There was peace between Heber and Jabin. Sisera, we are told, was a personal friend of Heber's.

Jael, Hebers wife, went out to meet Sisera, called him into her tent. When he asked for water she gave him milk and covered him. When he is sound asleep, Jael pounds a tent peg through his temple into the ground.

Barak was pursuing Sisera who had deserted his men and fled the scene. Jael went out to meet him and said, "Come on in. I will show you the man you're looking for."

In Judges 5, one of the most amazing victory songs in all of history is sung. Deborah and Barak sang together. Deborah, Barak, and Jael are honored. The song is a legacy to them for obedience to God regardless of who got the "glory" for the death blow to Sisera.

"And Barak said to her, 'If thou wilt go with me, I will go; and if thou wilt not go, I will not go; for I know not when the Lord prospers his messenger with me.'" This story is an excellent example of what a balance between the masculine and feminine can do when working together under God.

In any story in the Bible, one should pay particular attention to the names of the characters. They always reveal something about the personality, character, or roles played. In the above accounting,

Barak means "lightning sword"
Deborah means "to subdue, destroy, appoint, command, or declare"

Jael means "valuable, profitable, to do good"

Next, let us consider the word, Chayil, which is a Hebrew word occurring 242 times in the Old Testament. When used to describe men or groups made up of men, it is translated "army/war" 58 times, "host/force" 43 times, "might/power" 16 times, "goods/riches/wealth…" 30 times, "soldiers/training/ activity" 5 times, "valor" 28 times, "strength" 11 times, "valiant/valiantly" 35 times, "strong" 6 times, "able" 4 times, "worthily/ worthy" 2 times. The remaining 4 occurrences reference women.

Ruth 3:11 10 And he said, Blessed be thou of the Lord, my daughter: for thou hast shewed more kindness in the latter end than at the beginning, inasmuch as thou followedst not young men, whether poor or rich. 11 And now, my daughter, fear not; I will do to thee all that thou requirest: for all the city of my people doth know that thou art a virtuous woman.

The word "virtuous" is the same word, "chayil". Those who rendered the word for power and strength when used in conjunction with men render the same word as "virtuous" when relating it to women. However, the Septuagint does translate it in to the Greek word, "dunamis," which means "power".

Proverbs 31 King James Version (KJV)
31 The words of king Lemuel, the prophecy that his mother taught him.

2 What, my son? and what, the son of my womb? and what, the son of my vows?
3 Give not thy strength unto women, nor thy ways to that which destroyeth kings.
4 It is not for kings, O Lemuel, it is not for kings to

drink wine; nor for princes strong drink:

5 Lest they drink, and forget the law, and pervert the judgment of any of the afflicted.

6 Give strong drink unto him that is ready to perish, and wine unto those that be of heavy hearts.

7 Let him drink, and forget his poverty, and remember his misery no more.

8 Open thy mouth for the dumb in the cause of all such as are appointed to destruction.

9 Open thy mouth, judge righteously, and plead the cause of the poor and needy.

10 Who can find a virtuous woman? for her price is far above rubies.

The word "virtuous" is chayil. Who can find a strong, able woman? Her price is above rubies.

Let us look at the rest of this chapter and we shall let it prove the point and move on.

Proverbs 31: 11 The heart of her husband doth safely trust in her, so that he shall have no need of spoil.

12 She will do him good and not evil all the days of her

life.

13 She seeketh wool, and flax, and worketh willingly with her hands.

14 She is like the merchants' ships; she bringeth her food from afar.

15 She riseth also while it is yet night, and giveth meat to her household, and a portion to her maidens.

16 She considereth a field, and buyeth it: with the fruit of her hands she planteth a vineyard.

17 She girdeth her loins with strength, and strengtheneth her arms.

18 She perceiveth that her merchandise is good: her candle goeth not out by night.

19 She layeth her hands to the spindle, and her hands hold the distaff.

20 She stretcheth out her hand to the poor; yea, she reacheth forth her hands to the needy.

21 She is not afraid of the snow for her household: for all her household are clothed with scarlet.

22 She maketh herself coverings of tapestry; her clothing is silk and purple.

23 Her husband is known in the gates, when he sitteth

among the elders of the land.

24 She maketh fine linen, and selleth it; and delivereth girdles unto the merchant.

25 Strength and honour are her clothing; and she shall rejoice in time to come.

26 She openeth her mouth with wisdom; and in her tongue is the law of kindness.

27 She looketh well to the ways of her household, and eateth not the bread of idleness.

28 Her children arise up, and call her blessed; her husband also, and he praiseth her.

29 Many daughters have done virtuously, but thou excellest them all.

30 Favour is deceitful, and beauty is vain: but a woman that feareth the Lord, she shall be praised.

31 Give her of the fruit of her hands; and let her own works praise her in the gates.

Verse 29 is the summation of everything this woman embodies. She is strong, honorable, and efficient, yet the phrase chosen to sum up this woman is that she performed "virtuously." This word, is of course, "chayil". She has been strong, powerful, capable, valiant, and worthy. But, in the time this was being translated the highest value of a woman would be faithful and virtuous. Virtuous is a word defined as having high moral standards. The thesaurus equates the word to:

good, pure, whiter than white, saintly, angelic, moral, ethical, upright, upstanding, high-minded, principled, exemplary; law-abiding, irreproachable, blameless, guiltless, unimpeachable, immaculate, honest, honorable, reputable, laudable, decent, respectable, or noble. Strength and power are not in the list for women, but they are for men.

Who can find an able, strong, valiant, worthy women? If you do, she is worth rubies.

Joseph Lumpkin

What They Didn't Like, They Changed

Women in the New Testament are usually glossed over. In the beginning of the faith they had stations and positions; some ran churches out of their home; some were tireless workers; others were prophets. However, when the church fathers sat down to translate the New Testament, they did so in a way that diminished the strengths of the women. As the church moved from a grass-roots movement and became an organization it came under the control of men by great majority. This time began a history in which women were considered inferior by nature and by law.

These ideas were borrowed from Greek philosophy which held women to be inferior to men by nature. Roman law, which became the basis for the Church's laws, gave women a low status in society. Women did not enjoy equal rights in their homes and in civic society.

A minority of Fathers of the Church went so far as to link women's presumed inferior status to scriptural texts: only the man, they said, was created in God's image. Based on this view the more misogynistic male theologians actually believed since men were created directly by God only they were given souls. Paul seemed to follow the idea of female inferiority since he had forbidden women to teach in church. One explanation to Paul's decree was that women of the time were not educated. This may be true but would prove the point instead of defending it, see that women were not given the same education because their place in society was lower than that of men.

'Church Orders' of the first millennium also show traces of the belief in women's inferiority

Theologians too copied this line of thinking, integrating the anti-women views of Greeks and Romans into their theological reasoning.

Church lawyers formulated Church Law on the basis of Roman Law, and on the negative statements of Fathers and local Church Councils.

Yet, the Bible does in no way substantiates these twisted beliefs. One has only to glance through the scriptures to find women in roles and positions of leadership and power, and the tell-tale signs of the church's attempts to obfuscate the facts.

Romans 16 (KJV)

1) I commend unto you Phoebe our sister, which is a servant of the church which is at Cenchrea:

2) That ye receive her in the Lord, as becometh saints, and that ye assist her in whatsoever business she hath need of you: for she hath been a succourer of many, and of myself also.

The word translated here as "servant" is rendered as the word "deacon" for men in that position. Here, Phoebe is a servant. Being a woman who was running a church, Phoebe has always been a controversial figure. Paul calls Phoebe a prostatis (translated "succourer,"). The Greek noun used of Phoebe, prostatis, means "one standing before, a champion, leader, chief, or a protector." She stood before the people and she stood before God as being responsible for teaching and guiding those under her, both male and female.

In 1 Timothy 3:12, we read the following about Phoebe, in our English Bibles: "I commend unto you Phoebe our sister, minister [or deacon] of the church which is at Cenchrea; . . . for she hath been a ruler of many and of myself also." This is the noun form corresponding to the verb *prostatis,* translated "rule".

Let us look at the verses in context using the Amplified Bible, which attempts to clarify word meaning. Note all of the female names in the chapter.

Romans 16 (Amplified Bible)

1) Now, I introduce and commend to you our sister Phoebe, a deaconess of the church at Cenchreae,

2) That you may receive her in the Lord [with a

Christian welcome], as saints (God's people) ought to receive one another. And help her in whatever matter she may require assistance from you, for she has been a helper of many including myself [shielding us from suffering].

3) Give my greetings to Prisca and Aquila, my fellow workers in Christ Jesus,

4) Who risked their lives [endangering their very necks] for my life. To them not only I, but also all the churches among the Gentiles give thanks.

5) [Remember me] also to the church [that meets] in their house. Greet my beloved Epaenetus, who was a first fruit (first convert) to Christ in Asia.

6) Greet Mary, who has worked so hard among you.

7) Remember me to Andronicus and Junias, my tribal kinsmen and once my fellow prisoners. They are men held in high esteem among the apostles, who also were in Christ before I was.

8) Remember me to Ampliatus, my beloved in the Lord.

9) Salute Urbanus, our fellow worker in Christ, and my dear Stachys.

10) Greet Apelles, that one tried and approved in Christ (the Messiah). Remember me to those who belong to the household of Aristobulus.

11) Greet my tribal kinsman, Herodion, and those in the Lord who belong to the household of Narcissus.

12) Salute those workers in the Lord, Tryphaena and Tryphosa. Greet my dear Persis, who has worked so hard in the Lord.

13) Remember me to Rufus, eminent in the Lord, also to his mother [who has been] a mother to me as well.

14) Greet Asyncritus, Phlegon, Hermes, Patrobas, Hermas, and the brethren who are with them.

15) Greet Philologus, Julia, Nereus, and his sister, and Olympas, and all the saints who are with them.

16) Greet one another with a holy (consecrated) kiss. All the churches of Christ (the Messiah) wish to be remembered to you.

17) I appeal to you, brethren, to be on your guard concerning those who create dissensions and difficulties and cause divisions, in opposition to the doctrine (the teaching) which you have been taught. [I warn you to turn aside from them, to] avoid them.

18) For such persons do not serve our Lord Christ, but their own appetites and base desires, and by ingratiating and flattering speech, they beguile the hearts of the unsuspecting and simpleminded [people].

19) For while your loyalty and obedience is known to all, so that I rejoice over you, I would have you well versed and wise as to what is good and innocent and guileless as to what is evil.

20) And the God of peace will soon crush Satan under your feet. The grace of our Lord Jesus Christ (the Messiah) be with you.

21) Timothy, my fellow worker, wishes to be remembered to you, as do Lucius and Jason and Sosipater, my tribal kinsmen.

22) I, Tertius, the writer of this letter, greet you in the Lord.

23) Gaius, who is host to me and to the whole church here, greets you. So do Erastus, the city treasurer, and our brother Quartus.

24) The grace of our Lord Jesus Christ (the Messiah) be with you all. Amen (so be it).

25) Now to Him Who is able to strengthen you in the faith which is in accordance with my Gospel and the preaching of (concerning) Jesus Christ (the Messiah), according to the revelation (the unveiling) of the *mystery of the plan of redemption which was kept in silence and secret for long ages,*

26) *But is now disclosed and through the prophetic Scriptures is made known to all nations, according to the command of the eternal God, [to win them] to obedience to the faith,*

27) *To [the] only wise God be glory forevermore through Jesus Christ (the Anointed One)! Amen (so be it).*

Within the above text there are certain things that stand out. The first is the true rendering of the word "deaconess" in regard to Phoebe. The second is the positional listing of certain names. Prisca, also known as Priscilla, and Aquila, for example, shows that the woman, Prisca was likely in the position of authority in the writer's mind.

In I Timothy 3: 4, 5, 12; and 5:17, Paul tells men to "rule well" their own households. These men are told to "rule, champion, maintain" their households, as Paul tells us that Phoebe "ruled" him and many others. Phoebe held the same relation to the church at Cenchrea, that Paul says church officials should hold to their own children and household. We can see that the men should take good care of them, not "rule" them. These passages have no direct reference to rule, or government. In Titus 3:8, 14, the same word is translated "maintain." This is a better rendering of the word.

Now the Apostle Paul makes use of the verb form of this word in I Timothy 5:14 (KJV), "I will that the younger women marry, bear children, guide the house (oikodespotein), give none occasion to the adversary to speak reproachfully."

The Revised Version does the word a bit more justice and translates it, "rule the household." Is Paul saying the women are the authority of the home? In these times, the women were expected to run the household. Men did not have much to do with the daily decisions of household, children, or even the domestic help, such as slaves.

In Titus 2, Paul instructs the elder women to teach the young women to be "keepers at home". The Greek word translated "keepers at home" (KJV) or "homemakers" (NKJV) is oikouros. This compound word is from oikos- house, household, family; and a guard, guardian, a watcher, a warden. We think of a warden as a masculine position of authority.

It seems that our beliefs are colored by our society. One must attempt to take away the veil of looking at the 1611 society in which the King James' Version translators were immersed to find the truth. After the Geneva Bible and the King James' Bible were accepted as "The Word of God", other Bibles translations were expected to follow their meaning closely. Thus, many modern translators may see the truth more clearly than they can convey to the masses. Error propagates error, and the errors compound in time.

As a footnote, it is interesting to see that is Acts 18,

Priscilla instructs Apollos, the man who some think wrote the book of Hebrews. It is also possible that Priscilla contributed to the book of Hebrews, but these things are never clearly mentioned in the Bible and cannot be proven until further evidence is uncovered.

At times, those translating the Bible simply chose to do away with a woman by changing their name to that of a man.

In Romans 16:7, Paul praises a woman named Junia as "outstanding among the apostles."

KJV Romans 16:7 - "Salute Andronicus and Junia, my kinsmen, and my fellow-prisoners, who are of note among the apostles, who also were in Christ before me."

Note in the King James' Version the name, Junia, is a feminine name, but she is referred to as "kinsmen". Now, look at some other translations.

Young's Literal Translation (YLT)

Romans 16:7 - "salute Andronicus and Junias, my kindred, and my fellow-captives, who are of note among the apostles, who also have been in Christ before me."

New International Reader's Version (NIRV)

Romans 16:7 - Greet Andronicus and Junias, my relatives. They have been in prison with me. They are leaders among the apostles. They became believers in Christ before I did.

Bibles and commentators generally utilize Greek New Testaments in their translation and interpretive pursuit. The Greek source documents are given names and the copies are tracked like a family tree. Both the source documents UBS4 and NA27 Greek New Testaments show *Iounian* accented with a circumflex accent over the alpha, which indicates "Junias" as being a contracted form of Junianus, a male name. Support for "Junias" is attested to by B2 , D2, and a number of partial manuscripts dated from the 9th to 14th century.

No one translating or commenting on this verse prior to the 13th century questioned that this apostle was a woman. Before that time, most translations and copies agreed that Junia was a female who was called an apostle by Paul.

St. John Chrysostom wrote of Romans 16:7, "O how great is the devotion of this woman that she should be counted worthy of the appellation of apostle!"

Some time between the 9th and 13th century, as the church continued to oppress and diminish women, the idea of a female apostle became less tolerable and the verse was altered to fit the prevailing views of the time, an act that was done far more frequently than we would think.

Translators made up the name "Junias" to substitute for the actual name. However, the name that seemed to be the masculine form of the name they were attempting to eradicate was not a real name. No other person in any text has the name, Junias. This was an act she did not deserve. She was suffering along side the men in prison and was being tortured for the sake of the Gospel.

Early Christians under the oppression of Rome had to suffer to proclaim Jesus Christ as Lord. Junia and Andronicus, (perhaps her husband), were called apostles because they had suffered and were imprisoned.

According to Romans 16:7, Junia had become a convert of Jesus before Paul. Since Paul was converted just a few years after the Resurrection of Christ, Junia must have been one of the earliest converts to Christianity and could have been one of the founders of the church at Rome.

There was a sea-change or change of opinion in society between the times of the Old and New Testaments. The place of women in New

Testament society was limited. Jesus, being often found in the company of women, was looked at as odd and skating on the raw edge of what was permissible in society at the time. As we have read the stories of women in positions of authority, you will notice that most of them (not all, but most) come from the Old Testament. The place of women in society was becoming more and more limited. Their defined place in the Christian world would become subservient and meaningless. If a woman were to attempt to assert herself, it resulted in social upheaval and her being punished or becoming an outcast.

Although the idea of women being pastors fell into the social trap, which seems so often to ensnare the truth, it is very obvious in the early days of the church, women were not only included, but were some of the first pastors. John's greeting in his second letter did not address the church as the elect or chosen lady, as some would have us believe, but instead the greeting was to a specific woman, who was shepherding a church. Yes, she was a pastor.

What's more, the letter is so personal that it was addressed to her, not by the general salutation of "chosen by God", but by her name, which means "chosen by God." My name is Joseph, which means, "he shall add." Her name was Kyria, which is a feminine form of, "one who is chosen or elected by God."   When rendered into an English version the name is "Electa."

Kyria, or Electa, has been swept under the rug where the church sweeps ideas they wish would go quietly into the night. Women in the priesthood? John had no problem with it.

Let's look at the modern NIV translation and then compare it to two older, more literal translations.

2 John 1
New International Version (NIV)

1) The elder,

To the lady chosen by God and to her children, whom I love in the truth—and not I only, but also all who know the truth—

2) because of the truth, which lives in us and will be with us forever:

2 John 1
Young's Literal Translation (YLT)

1) The Elder to the choice Kyria, and to her children, whom I love in truth, and not I only, but also all those having known the truth,

2) because of the truth that is remaining in us, and with us shall be to the age,

2 John 1:5
and now I beseech thee, Kyria, not as writing to thee a new command, but which we had from the beginning, that we may love one another, (YLT

2 John 1
Wycliffe New Testament (WYC)

1) The elder man, to the chosen lady [The elder man to the lady Electa], and to her children, which I love in truth; and not I alone, but also all men that know truth [but and all men that knew truth]...

I ask you, who are we to argue with the apostle, John?

There were women who were warriors. There were women who were prophets. There were women who were deacons. There were women who were pastors. It was a group of women who funded the ministry of Jesus. The first person to whom the resurrection was revealed was a woman. In the beginning of the Christian faith women were the backbone of the new sect. Yet, by the time the Bible was being compiled into a standard book, women were so marginalized that they could no longer be leaders, deacon or pastors. They had their place in society, which had limited their position in the church. They were to be kept behind the scene and let the men lead. At this point in what was viewed as the social norms it is no wonder any text, which contained a strong, will, self determined woman would have been excluded from the Bible. Such was the disposition of the Acts of Paul and Thecla. Even if the majority of church fathers would have considered the book authentic, and even if a written version could have been found originating from the time of the apostles, this book would have been excluded. Thecla was much to strong for the existing society, and she preached celibacy, even to the point of wives being disobedient to her husband.

Joseph Lumpkin

Too Strong for the Bible

By the time texts were being selected for inclusion in the New Testament, entire books were being culled due to their disruptive messages. If books were theologically sound, but caused one to question the authority of men, it was excluded from the Bible. There was to be no contamination of the masses with foreign ideas, such as females being in positions of leadership or authority in the church or in life.

Presented here is one such book, whose theme was so disturbing that it was rejected off hand. The story of Paul and Thecla is a well-known book among Bible scholars. The messages being proclaimed by "The Acts of Paul and Thecla", was one where a woman was a healer, evangelist, preacher, and leader. She baptized without asking for the authority or consent of a man. She was also a virgin who caused havoc by refusing to marry, deciding instead to help spread the Gospel.

The abstinence from coitus is a theme running throughout the texts, as Thecla fights to keep her virginity by refusing to marry after hearing a sermon by Paul urging purity, chastity, and abstinence. Paul urges both the unmarried person and married couples to keep themselves pure, following God, praying, and rejecting the pleasures of the world. As Paul travels, Thecla joins him in his mission, but departs from his company from time to time to teach and heal, without the assistance or permission of Paul. Time and time again Thecla or Paul upset town's folk with their messages. Over and over again Thecla or Paul were ejected from one city after another.

The abrupt beginning or the story indicates in was likely taken from a larger work that was circulating earlier. There was a body of work attributed to Paul during the first and second centuries CE. The story makes for interesting reading and serves as a lesson on how to be excluded from the Bible by challenging the current institutions of power and gender.

The first of the Fathers to mention the Acts of Paul and Thecla is Tertullian, who inveighed against it on the ground of its advocacy of the rights of women to preach and to baptize. Tertullian seeks to overthrow the authority of the work by alleging that its author was a presbyter of Asia Minor who confessed to having forged the story from love of Paul, and who had been deposed from office in consequence.

Tertullian says that a Presbyter of Asia, who being convicted, "confessed that he did it out of respect of Paul," forged this piece and Pope Gelasius, in his Decree against apocryphal books, inserted it among them. Notwithstanding this, a large part of the history was credited, and looked upon as genuine among the primitive Christians. Cyprian, Eusebius, Epiphanius, Austin, Gregory Nazianzen, Chrysostom, and Severus Sulpitius, who all lived within the fourth century, mention Thecla, or refer to her history. Basil of Seleucia wrote her acts, sufferings, and victories, in verse; and Euagrius Scholasticus, an ecclesiastical historian, living around 590 C.E. relates that "after the Emperor Zeno had abdicated his empire, and Basilik had taken possession of it, he had a vision of the holy and excellent martyr Thecla, who promised him the restoration of his empire; for which, when it was brought about, he erected and dedicated a most noble and sumptuous temple to this famous martyr Thecla, at Seleucia, a city of Isauria, and bestowed upon it very noble endowments, which, according to the author are "preserved even till this day." Hist. Eccl., lib. 3, cap.

Cardinal Baronius, Locrinus, Archbishop Wake, and others; and also the learned Grabe, who edited the Septuagint, and revived the Acts of Paul and Thecla, consider them as having been written in the Apostolic age; as containing nothing superstitious, or disagreeing from the opinions and belief of those times; and, in short, as a genuine and authentic history. Again, it is said, that this is not the original book of the early Christians; but however that may be, it is published from the Greek MS. in the Bodleian Library at Oxford, which Dr. Mills copied and transmitted to Dr. Grabe.

The Acts of Paul and Thecla is a religious romance. In the text Thecla is transfixed with Paul's teaching. Some translations say she was in ecstasy. It is here she fell in love with God and from that time forward she wish for no one to touch her but God. He chastity was wrapped up in this ideal relationship. The Acts of Paul and Thecla was part of that larger work. The text had already been separated from a larger work and was in common use when Tertullian wrote about it.

The story was written probably in the latter part of the second century — Harnack would say between 160 and 170 A. D. in Asia Minor. The year 190 A.D. is given as the latest date the book could have been written.

Its purpose was clearly threefold: first, to defend the apostle against his Ebionites, who were slandering Paul with their hints of personal attachment to his women converts.

The word Ebionites, or rather, more correctly, Ebionæans (Ebionaioi), is a transliteration of an Aramean word meaning "poor men". Origen (Against Celsus II.1; De Princ., IV, i, 22) and Eusebius (Church History III.27) refer the name of these sectaries either to the poverty of their understanding, or to the poverty of the Law to which they clung, or to the poor opinions they held concerning Christ. The doctrines of this sect are said by Irenaeus to be like those of Cerinthus and Carpocrates. They denied the Divinity and the virginal birth of Christ; they clung to the observance of the Jewish Law; they regarded St. Paul as an apostate, and used only a Gospel according to St. Matthew (Adv. Haer., I, xxvi, 2; III, xxi, 2; IV, xxxiii, 4; V, i, 3). Some Ebionites accept, but others reject, the virginal birth of Christ, though all reject His pre-existence and His Divinity. Those who accepted the virginal birth seem to have had more exalted views concerning Christ and, besides observing the Sabbath, to have kept the Sunday as a memorial of His Resurrection.

The second reason for the writing of The Acts of Paul and Thecla was to bolster the practice of virginity and celibacy within the church. This practice seems to have started with ideas of Plato, which found their way into the church. Part of the reason for celibacy in western culture is no doubt due to Plato, the ancient Greek philosopher. Though he lived over 300 before the birth of Christ, Plato laid the foundations of western philosophy and created, in part, the intellectual background in which the New Testament was written. Many Church Fathers found deep connections between Plato's thought and divine revelation, and that many of Plato's ideas were helpful in explaining Christian doctrine. In fact, Justin Martyr, the Cappadocian Fathers, Augustine, and Eusebius all pointed to Plato's philosophy as confirmation of what St. Paul wrote at the beginning of Romans, that God's eternal power and divine nature can be seen understood by reflecting on the world that he has made.

To begin with, Jesus designated St. Peter, a married man, to be the first pope. Priests had married in Judaism (the priesthood itself was a hereditary profession), and it would seem that Christ accepted this part of the tradition in his choice of Peter. Although St. Paul believed that spreading the Gospel was easier for a man who didn't have a family to provide for, he still mandated that bishops, elders and deacons be only "the husband of one wife." The comment about a single wife was because at that time polygamy among all ranks of the clergy persisted. By the third century bishops alone were required to be monogamous.

As the influence of Plato continued to be felt with the church the idea of celibacy continued to creep in. In the end it was greed that pushed the church to demand celibacy from its priests. A married priest would pass down his wealth and land to his children. A celibate priest would leave his wealth and land to the church.

The change began with the Council of Elvira in Spain in about 306, which prohibited bishops, deacons and priests from marrying. Shortly thereafter, the early church fathers began to stigmatize sex as sinful in their writings. St. Ambrose (340-397) wrote, "The ministerial office must be kept pure and unspoiled and must not be defiled by coitus," and the former libertine St. Augustine (354-430) even went so far as to consider an erect penis a sign of man's insubordination to God.

The third reason The Acts of Paul and Thecla was written could have been to assert the right of women to preach and to baptize.

From the beginning of Jesus' ministry women

played a vital part. Luke 8 tells us it was a group of women that financially supported Jesus.

Luke 8 Holman Christian Standard Bible (HCSB)
8:1 Soon afterward He was traveling from one town and village to another, preaching and telling the good news of the kingdom of God. The Twelve were with Him, 2 and also some women who had been healed of evil spirits and sicknesses: Mary, called Magdalene (seven demons had come out of her); 3 Joanna the wife of Chuza, Herod's steward; Susanna; and many others who were supporting them from their possessions.

Based on the elevation of the position and leadership of women taught in the Acts of Paul and Thecla, it is easy to see why the church would wish to ignore the book and not consider it's inclusion as canon. By the time canon was being established the church had become an organization controlled only by men.

The Acts of Paul and Thecla is a story in which the first scene opens in Asia Minor. Paul is on one of his evangelizing tours in Lycaonia, and with two companions, Demas and Hermogenes as they approach the city of Iconium. The city, now called Konya (Turkish pronunciation: ['kon.ja]; Greek: Ικόνιον Ikónion, Latin: Iconium) is a city in the Central Anatolia Region of Turkey. Today it is the seventh most populous city in Turkey.

As the scene opens, Paul's personal appearance is described with such circumstantial detail as to suggest that it may be in part an authentic tradition. It certainly seems the author describing the apostle did not idealize him.

" In stature," says the Syriac, " he was a man of middling size, and his hair was scanty, and his legs were a little crooked, and his knees were projecting, and he had large [the Armenian says "blue"] eyes, and his eyebrows met, and his nose was somewhat long, and he was full of grace and mercy ; at one time he seemed like a man, and at another time he seemed like an angel."

An Iconian named Onesiphorus, with his wife and sons meet Paul and recognize him by this description, which Titus has given them.

Onesiphorus takes Paul to his house and entertains him. There, after prayer and the breaking of bread, Paul presents his doctrine on virginity in a series of beatitudes.

From the window of an adjoining house a maiden named Thecla, who was betrothed to a man named Thamyris, overhears Paul's words. Thecla is fascinated by his teaching and is transfixed, listening from the window.

Alarmed at this her mother summons Thamyris, and tells him how for three days Thecla has not eaten nor drunk, but remained at her window. They both labor with her, to no purpose. On leaving the house, Thamyris, now greatly incensed, encounters Paul's companions, Demas and Hermogenes. He offers them money for information against Paul, and entertains them sumptuously. The men explain the virginity teaching and advise Thamyris to have Paul before the prefect on the charge of teaching a new doctrine and being a Christian. Accordingly the next day Paul is seized by Thamyris and his associates and brought before the prefect, by whom he is examined and committed to prison.

In his prison he is visited by Thecla, who escapes by night from her mother's house by bribing the doorkeeper with her bracelets, and gains admission to the prison by giving the jailer her silver mirror. In the prison she listens joyfully to the teachings of Paul, sitting at his feet and kissing his fetters.

Meanwhile her family and her betrothed, aroused by her disappearance, are searching the city for her. The confession of the doorkeeper reveals her whereabouts, and her friends surprise her listening in the prison, with many others, to the apostle's preaching. They inform the prefect. He orders Paul and Thecla to be brought before him. Paul is scourged and cast out of the city, but Thecla, at her mother's instance, is condemned to be burned. The pile of fagots is prepared in the theater, and Thecla, encouraged by a vision of the Lord, stretches out her hands in the form of the cross and ascends the pile. But no sooner is the torch applied than a flood of rain extinguishes the fire, and Thecla is delivered.

Meantime Paul, whose exile is shared by Onesiphorus and his family, has taken refuge in a wayside tomb near the city.

They had been long fasting, and had nothing to buy food with, so Paul striped off his tunic, and sent it by a boy to the city. The Greek version says they went, "on the road by which they go from Iconium to Daphne." Critics believe there was confusion between the Pisidian Antioch and the Syrian Antioch. The latter, it is well known, had a Daphne in its vicinity. Daphne is not mentioned in the Syriac, Armenian, or Ethiopian text.

The Greek text tells us the boy sold the cloak or simply exchanged it for bread. This boy then meets Thecla coming out of the city, and conducted her to Paul's hiding-place. She found Paul praying for her deliverance from the flames, and dramatically responded with a prayer of thanksgiving for her preservation, to which Paul rejoined the others with a prayer of praise. After they had eaten, Thecla announced that she wished to cut off her hair and follow Paul as his attendant. She asked for the seal of baptism. Paul tells her to be patient. Onesiphorus and his family then returned to Iconium, and Paul and Thecla set off for Antioch.

In Antioch a certain Alexander, one of the chief men of the city, was giving public spectacles. Alexander sees Thecla with Paul, and, being enamored of her, tries to buy her from Paul.

Paul protests that she is not his, and Alexander thereupon embraces her in the public street. She indignantly resists, tearing his festal garments and ripping from his head his crown of gold leaves with the image of the emperor. Alexander denounces her to the prefect, who examines her and, upon her confession of what she has done, condemns her to be thrown to the beasts. The ground for this seems to have been the insult to the divinity of the emperor, implied in the removal and destruction of Alexander's wreath.

Upon Thecla's petition that she be kept in purity until her execution, she is placed in the keeping of Queen Tryphsena, a cousin of the emperor Claudius. The queen, who has lately lost a daughter, finds consolation in the society of Thecla and conceives a great affection for her.

The time appointed for Thecla's execution having arrived, she is brought into the theater and bound to a huge lioness.

But the beast, instead of rending her, licks her feet. Queen Tryphaena, moved by a vision of her daughter, takes Thecla again to her house until the next day, when she is exposed a second time to the beasts. Again they are powerless against her. A savage lioness takes up its position at her feet and defends her, killing a lion and a bear that are set upon her.

While fresh beasts are being brought in, Thecla baptizes herself in the seal tank in the theater. The women among the spectators, filled with sympathy for Thecla, fling perfumes upon her.

Ramsay, "The Church in the Roman Empire", pp. 375-428 ; and Conybeare, "The Acts of Apollonius", etc., pp. 49 report the following;

Besides the Greek form of the romance, which is probably generally the original form, there are Syriac, Latin, Armenian, Coptic, and Ethiopic versions, which sometimes diverge strikingly from the representation of the Greek. Thus much that

Professor Ramsay has thought anachronistic in the Greek form disappears in the Armenian, while in the Ethiopic, with the omission of Thecla's admitted claim to preach and to baptize, half the point of the story is lost.

The fresh beasts, instead of attacking Thecla, fall asleep about her. As a last resort she is bound to two savage bulls, and fiery spits are applied to them to infuriate them. But the fiery spits burn off the cords that bind Thecla, and she thus escapes the bulls.

At this point Queen Tryphaena, who has been a horrified observer of these ordeals, faints away. A report that she is dead is started by her slaves, and soon reaches the governor. The games are stopped, and at Alexander's express entreaty Thecla is released. She publicly ascribes her preservation to God, declaring herself his handmaiden, and the women of the city greet her release with acclamations and shouts of praise to him.

Queen Tryphaena hails her as her daughter and takes her to her house, where Thecla's preaching leads the queen and many of her maidens to believe.

Released from her difficulties Thecla resumes her search for Paul. Learning that he is in Myra, she disguises herself as a man, and with an escort from Queen Tryphsena's household goes from there out in search of him. She finds him and narrates to him all her experiences, beginning with her baptism of herself in the theater. All join in thanksgiving over her repeated deliverances. She declares to Paul her intention to return to Iconium, and he replies with the words, which give these Acts their chief significance: "Go and teach there the commandments of God."

With this commission Thecla returns to Iconium. She learns that Thamyris is dead, but meets Onesiphorus and her mother, before whom she bears eloquent testimony to her new faith. Then, departing from Iconium, she takes up her abode in Seleucia, where, after a life devoted to the religious enlightenment of the people, she falls asleep.

The condemnation of anyone merely on the charge of being a Christian is more natural in the days of Antoninus or Marcus Aurelius than earlier, and the entire absence of Jews from the list of the persecutors of Paul and Thecla betrays a late stage in the life of the early church. In Demas and Hermogenes we have perhaps the slightly veiled impersonations of Gnostic error, which again, though of course nowhere explicitly mentioned, is combated in Paul's preaching in these Acts. While the most critical scholarship has favored a date in the latter half of the second century, and the recent discovery of these Acts in the Acts of Paul has greatly strengthened this position, one must not lose sight of the fact that there are some evidences of exact topographical and historical information as to Lycaonia in the time of Paul that argue for some elements of tradition in the Acts of Paul and Thecla having an origin in the first century. Professor Ramsay has skillfully detected these.

"The popularity of this singular romance is well attested and easily understood. Its early separation from the parent Acts of Paul, the selection of it by Tertullian as an object of attack, and its translation, as a separate work, into many languages, illustrate its popularity; and in times when the celibate life was growing in popular favor, when marvelous martyrdoms were increasingly in demand, and when old men and maidens were the favorite figures among Christian confessors, popularity for a work like the Acts of Paul and Thecla was natural and inevitable. "

This ends the notes of Ramsay, The Church in the Roman Empire, pp. 375-428 ; and Conybeare, The Acts of Apollonius, etc., pp. 49.

Having covered the history and overview of the story, let us now look at the text itself.

Commentary and notes are in italicized font.

THE ACTS OF PAUL AND THECLA

Chapter I

1) When Paul went up to Iconium, after his flight from Antioch, Demas and Hermogenes became his companions, who were then full of hypocrisy.

2) But Paul, looking only at the goodness of God, did them no harm, but loved them greatly.

3) Accordingly he endeavored to make agreeable to them all the oracles and doctrines of Christ, and the design of the Gospel of God's well-beloved Son, instructing them in the knowledge of Christ, as it was revealed to him.

One of the incidents at Antioch was an Apostolic Age dispute between the apostles Paul and Peter, which occurred in the city of Antioch around the middle of the first century. The primary source for the incident is Paul's Epistle to the Galatians 2:11–14. Paul was in opposition to the leadership of James and Peter, bringing conflict among the leaders of Early Christianity. Among the points of disagreement was whether Christians had to become Jews first, if they needed to be circumcised, and what laws new Christians must follow. The final outcome of the incident remains uncertain resulting in several Christian views of the Old Covenant to this day.

Galatians 2 Holman Christian Standard Bible (HCSB)

Paul Defends His Gospel at Jerusalem

2 Then after 14 years I went up again to Jerusalem with Barnabas, taking Titus along also. 2 I went up according to a revelation and presented to them the gospel I preach among the Gentiles — but privately to those recognized as leaders — so that I might not be running, or have run the race, in vain. 3 But not even Titus who was with me, though he was a Greek, was compelled to be circumcised. 4 This issue arose because of false brothers smuggled in, who came in secretly to spy on the freedom that we have in Christ Jesus, in order to enslave us. 5 But we did not give up and submit to these people for even an hour, so that the truth of the gospel would be preserved for you.

6 Now from those recognized as important (what they really were makes no difference to me; God does not show favoritism [a]) — they added nothing to me. 7 On the contrary, they saw that I had been entrusted with the gospel for the uncircumcised, just as Peter was for the circumcised, 8 since the One at work in Peter for an apostleship to the circumcised was also at work in me for the Gentiles. 9 When James, Cephas, and John, recognized as pillars, acknowledged the grace that had been given to me, they gave the right hand of fellowship to me and Barnabas, agreeing that we should go to the Gentiles and they to the circumcised. 10 They asked only that we would remember the poor, which I made every effort to do.

Freedom from the Law

11 But when Cephas came to Antioch, I opposed him to his face because he stood condemned. 12 For he regularly ate with the Gentiles before certain men came from James. However, when they came, he withdrew and separated himself, because he feared those from the circumcision party. 13 Then the rest of the Jews joined his hypocrisy, so that even Barnabas was carried away by their hypocrisy. 14 But when I saw that they were

deviating from the truth of the gospel, I told Cephas in front of everyone, "If you, who are a Jew, live like a Gentile and not like a Jew, how can you compel Gentiles to live like Jews?"

15 We who are Jews by birth and not "Gentile sinners" 16 know that no one is justified by the works of the law but by faith in Jesus Christ. And we have believed in Christ Jesus so that we might be justified by faith in Christ and not by the works of the law, because by the works of the law no human being will be justified. 17 But if we ourselves are also found to be "sinners" while seeking to be justified by Christ, is Christ then a promoter of sin? Absolutely not! 18 If I rebuild the system I tore down, I show myself to be a lawbreaker. 19 For through the law I have died to the law, so that I might live for God. I have been crucified with Christ 20 and I no longer live, but Christ lives in me. The life I now live in the body, I live by faith in the Son of God, who loved me and gave Himself for me. 21 I do not set aside the grace of God, for if righteousness comes through the law, then Christ died for nothing.

Footnotes:

Chapter 1:4) And a certain man named Onesiphorus, hearing that Paul was come to Iconium, went out speedily to meet him, together with his wife Lectra, and his sons Simmia and Xeno, to invite him to their house.

5) For Titus had given them a description of Paul's personage, they as yet not knowing him in person, but only being acquainted with his character.

6) They went in the king's highway to Lystra, and stood there waiting for him, comparing all who passed by, with that description which Titus had given them.

7) At length, they saw a man coming (namely Paul), of a short stature, with a bald head, crooked thighs, strong legs, hollow-eyed (one source says blue eyes); had a crooked nose; full of grace; for sometimes he appeared as a man, sometimes he had the countenance of an angel. And Paul saw Onesiphorus, and was glad.

8) And Onesiphorus said: "Hail, thou servant of the blessed God." Paul replied, "The grace of God be

with thee and thy family."

9) But Demas and Hermogenes were moved with envy, and, under a show of great religion, Demas said, "And are not we also servants of the blessed God? Why didst thou not salute us?"

10) Onesiphorus replied, "Because I have not perceived in you the fruits of righteousness; nevertheless, if ye are of that sort, ye shall be welcome to my house also."

11) Then Paul went into the house of Onesiphorus, and there was great joy among the family on that account: and they employed themselves in prayer, breaking of bread, and hearing Paul preach the word of God concerning the temperance and the resurrection, in the following manner:

12) Blessed are the pure in heart; for they shall see God.

13) Blessed are they who keep their flesh undefiled (or pure); for they shall be the temple of God.

14) Blessed are the temperate (or chaste); for God will reveal himself to them.

15) Blessed are they who abandon their secular enjoyments for they shall be accepted of God.

16) Blessed are they who have wives, as though they had them not; for they shall be made angels of God.

17) Blessed are they who tremble at the word of God; for they shall be comforted.

18) Blessed are they who keep their baptism pure; for they shall find peace with the Father, Son, and Holy Ghost.

19) Blessed are they who pursue the wisdom (or doctrine) of Jesus Christ; for they shall be called the sons of the Most High.

20) Blessed are they who observe the instructions of Jesus Christ; for they shall dwell in eternal light.

21) Blessed are they, who for the love of Christ abandon the glories of the world; for they shall judge angels, and be placed at the right hand of Christ, and shall not suffer the bitterness of the last judgment.

22) Blessed are the bodies and souls of virgins; for they are acceptable to God, and shall not lose the reward of their virginity; for the word of their (heavenly) Father shall prove effectual to their

salvation in the day of his Son, and they shall enjoy rest for evermore.

Chapter II

1) While Paul was preaching this sermon in the church which was in the house of Onesiphorus, a certain virgin, named Thecla (whose mother's name was Theoclia, and who was betrothed to a man named Thamyris) sat at a certain window in her house.

2) By the placement and position (advantage) of a window in the house where Paul was, she heard Paul's sermons both night and day concerning God, charity, faith in Christ, and concerning prayer;

3) And Thecla would not depart from the window, until she was overtaken with ecstasy (great joy), transfixed, having heard the doctrines of faith.

4) Over a period of time she saw many women and virgins going in to Paul and she earnestly desired that she might be thought worthy to appear in his presence, and hear the word of Christ; for she had not yet seen Paul in person, but only heard his sermons, and that alone.

5) But when she would not be persuaded to depart from the window, her mother sent to Thamyris, who came with the greatest pleasure, because he was hoping to marry her. Accordingly he said to Theoclia, "Where is my Thecla?"

The following discourse is spoken by Thecla's mother and is in third person, as she tells Thamyris about what is happening to Thecla.

6) Theoclia replied, "Thamyris, I have something very strange to tell you. For the space of three days Thecla, would not move from the window, not even to eat or drink, but was so intent on hearing the artful and deceitfully convincing discourses of a certain foreigner, that she perfectly admires, Thamyris, and he has convinced her that she now wonders how a young woman of known modesty and virginity could be so ill-treated.

7) For that man has disturbed the whole city of Iconium, and even your Thecla, among others. All the women and young men flock to him to receive

his doctrine. In addition to all his teachings he tells them that there is but one God, who alone is to be worshipped, and that we ought to live in chastity.

8) This is why, my daughter Thecla, was like a spider's web, fastened to the window, and captivated by the discourses of Paul, and attends upon his words with the utmost eagerness, and great delight; and so by listening to what he says, the young woman is seduced. Now then you should go and speak to her, for she is betrothed to you."

9) Accordingly Thamyris went, and having saluted (kissed) her, and taking care not to surprise her, he said, "Thecla, my spouse, why do you sit in this melancholy state? What strange impressions are made upon you? Turn to Thamyris, and be ashamed of yourself."

10) Her mother also spoke to her after the same manner, and said, "Child, why do you sit so melancholy, and, like one astonished, make no reply?"

11) Then they wept exceedingly: Thamyris, that he

84

had lost his spouse; Theoclia, that she had lost her daughter; and the maids, that they had lost their mistress; and there was an universal mourning in the family.

12) But all these things made no impression upon Thecla, and she did not even look at them or take notice of them, because she was still listening the discourses of Paul.

13) Then Thamyris ran out into the street to observe who they were who went into Paul, and came out from him; and he saw two men engaged in a very lively discussion, and said to them;

14) "Sirs, what business have you here? and who is that man within, belonging to you, who deludes the minds of men, both young men and virgins, persuading them, that they ought not to marry, but continue as they are?"

15) "I promise to give you a considerable sum (of money), if you will give me a truthful account of him; for I am the chief person of this city."

16) Demas and Hermogenes replied, "We cannot so exactly tell who he is; but this we know, that he

deprives young men of their (intended) wives, and virgins of their (intended) husbands, by teaching them that there can be no future resurrection, unless you continue in chastity, and do not defile your flesh."

The original leaders of the Christian movement, such as James, wished to keep the new Christian movement closer to its Jewish roots and as such they took the commandment from God to "be fruitful and multiply" very seriously. They expected followers to marry and to have children. Paul, apparently, had other ideas. Beginning with a statement in the New Testament that, it would be better if a man did not marry, he increases his opposition to marriage and sex in this book, thus alienating much of the population.

1 Corinthians 7 Holman Christian Standard Bible (HCSB)
Principles of Marriage
7 Now in response to the matters you wrote about: "It is good for a man not to have relations with a woman." 2 But because sexual immorality is so common, each man

should have his own wife, and each woman should have her own husband. 3 A husband should fulfill his marital responsibility to his wife, and likewise a wife to her husband. 4 A wife does not have the right over her own body, but her husband does. In the same way, a husband does not have the right over his own body, but his wife does. 5 Do not deprive one another sexually — except when you agree for a time, to devote yourselves to prayer. Then come together again; otherwise, Satan may tempt you because of your lack of self-control. 6 I say the following as a concession, not as a command. 7 I wish that all people were just like me. But each has his own gift from God, one person in this way and another in that way.

A Word to the Unmarried

8 I say to the unmarried and to widows: It is good for them if they remain as I am. 9 But if they do not have self-control, they should marry, for it is better to marry than to burn with desire.

Chapter III

1) Then Thamyris said, "Come along with me to my house, and refresh yourselves." So they went to a very lavish party, where there was wine in abundance, and very sumptuous food.

2) They were brought to a table richly spread, and made to drink plentifully by Thamyris, on account of the love he had for Thecla and his desire to marry her.

3) Then Thamyris said, "I would like for you to inform me what the doctrines of this Paul are, that I may understand them; for I am very concerned about Thecla, seeing she so delights in that stranger's discourses, that I am in danger of losing my intended wife."

4) Then Demas and Hermogenes answered both together, and said, "Let him be brought before the governor Castillius, as one who endeavors to persuade the people into the new religion of the Christians, and he, according to the order of Caesar, will put him to death. This will ensure you will obtain your wife;

5) While we at the same time will teach her, that the

resurrection which he speaks of is already come, and consists in our having children; and that we then arose again, when we came to the knowledge of God."

This is a rather Gnostic interpretation of the doctrine of resurrection that maintains there is no literal physical resurrection but rather a "spiritual resurrection" is obtained when one is "saved" or brought into the knowledge of God, which Jesus was sent to impart.

6) Thamyris having this account from them, was filled with hot resentment:

7) And rising early in the morning, he went to the house of Onesiphorus, attended by the magistrates, the jailer, and a great multitude of people with staves, and said to Paul;

8) "You have perverted the city of Iconium, and among the rest, Thecla, who is betrothed to me, so that now she will not marry me. You shall therefore go with us to the governor Castillius."

9) And the entire multitude cried out, "Away with this sorcerer, for he has perverted the minds of our wives, and all the people hearken to him."

Chapter IV

1) Then Thamyris, standing before the governor's judgment-seat, spoke with a loud voice in the following manner.

2) "O governor, I know not from where this man came; but he is one who teaches that matrimony is unlawful. Command him therefore to declare before you for what reason he teaches such doctrines to the people."

3) While he was saying thus, Demas and Hermogenes whispered to Thamyris, and) said; "Say that he is a Christian, and he will presently be put to death."

4) But the governor was more deliberate, and calling to Paul, he said, "Who are you? What do you teach? They seem to charge you with great and high crimes."

5) Paul then spoke with a loud voice, saying, "As I am now called to give an account, O governor, of

my doctrines, I desire your audience.

6) That God, who is a God of vengeance, and who stands in need of nothing but the salvation of his creatures, has sent me to reclaim them from their wickedness and corruptions, from all sinful pleasures, and from death; and to persuade them to sin no more.

7) For this purpose, God sent his Son Jesus Christ, whom I preach, and in whom I instruct men to place their hopes, as that person who only had such compassion on the deluded world, that it might not, O governor, be condemned, but have faith, the fear of God, the knowledge of religion, and the love of truth.

8) So that if I only teach those things which I have received by revelation from God, where is my crime?"

Note here that Paul specifically states he received his knowledge and doctrine by revelation. This is because unlike the leaders of the church at the time, Paul never actually met Jesus. He claimed that he communed with risen Jesus and received teaching in this way. This is the way his doctrine differed from that of the original church leaders who had been with Jesus. In spite of this, Paul condemns all other doctrines but his own.

Galatians 1: 9 As we said before, so say I now again, If any man preach any other gospel unto you than that ye have received, let him be accursed.

10 For do I now persuade men, or God? Or do I seek to please men? For if I yet pleased men, I should not be the servant of Christ.

11 But I certify you, brethren that the gospel, which was preached of me, is not after man.

12 For I neither received it of man, neither was I taught it, but by the revelation of Jesus Christ.

9) When the governor heard this, he ordered Paul to be bound, and to be put in prison till he should be more at leisure to hear him more fully.

10) But in the night, Thecla took off her earrings and gave them to the keeper of the keys of the prison, who then opened the doors to her, and let

her in;

11) And when she made a present of a silver mirror to the jailer, she was allowed to go into the room where Paul was. Then she sat down at his feet, and heard from him the great things of God.

12) And as she perceived Paul not to be afraid of suffering, but that by divine assistance he conducted himself with courage, her faith increased so greatly that she kissed his chains.

Chapter V

1) After a while Thecla was missed, and sought for by the family and by Thamyris in every street, as though she had been lost, but one of the porter's fellow-servants told them, that she had gone out in the nighttime.

2) Then they questioned the porter, and he told them, that she was gone to the prison to the stranger.

3) They went, therefore, according to his direction, and there they found her; and when they came out, they gathered a mob together, and went and told

the governor all that happened.

4) Upon which he ordered Paul to be brought before his judgment seat.

5) Thecla, in the mean time, lay wallowing on the ground in the prison, in that same place where Paul had sat to teach her; upon which the governor also ordered her to be brought before his judgment-seat; which summons she received with joy, and went.

It is not clear if Thecla was "wallowing" in a place she believed to be sacred because Paul was there or if she was protesting Paul's treatment, but the first assumption seems to hold with the storyline.

6) When Paul was brought out, the mob with more vehemence cried out, "He is a sorcerer, let him be killed."

7) Nevertheless, the governor listened with pleasure to Paul's discourses of the holy works of Christ; and, after he had concluded his interrogations, he summoned Thecla, and said to her, "Why do you not act according to the law of

the Iconians and marry Thamyris?"

8) She stood still, with her eyes fixed upon Paul; and finding she made no reply, Theoclia, her mother, cried out, saying, "Let the unjust creature be burnt; let her be burnt in the midst of the theatre, for refusing Thamyris, that all women may learn from her to avoid such practices."

As we attempt to "place flesh and blood" on the story in order to understand the human reasons for actions taken in this tale we have to pause here and ask why a mother would demand that her own daughter be burned alive in the middle of the city, in an open, public coliseum, for all to witness. Was her mother enraged by Thecla's defiance to custom? Is this the case of one generation hating the next? Is the mother attempting to distance herself from the insolence of her daughter in order to spare herself from any repercussions? We may never know why Thecla's mother reacted so violently to her actions, but we must ask ourselves how we react to the rebellion of a younger generation as it opposes our dearly held customs and beliefs.

9) Then the governor was exceedingly concerned, and ordered Paul to be taken outside the city and whipped, and for Thecla to be burnt alive.

10) So the governor arose, and went immediately into the theatre; and all the people went out to see the miserable, morose sight.

11) Just as a lamb in the wilderness looks every way to see his shepherd, Thecla looked around for Paul;

12) And as she was looking upon the multitude, she saw the Lord Jesus in the likeness of Paul, and said to herself, Paul has come to see me in my distressed circumstances. And she fixed her eyes upon him; but he instantly ascended up to heaven, while she watched him.

From the statement that Thecla was watching for Paul, we conclude that after being beaten, Paul was released. This will be confirmed later as we learn that Paul had fled to a cave outside the city.

13) The young men and women brought wood and

straw for the burning of Thecla. And she was brought naked to the stake. But the sight of her brought tears to the eyes of the governor, because he was surprised as he beheld the greatness of her beauty.

14) And when they had placed the wood in the proper pattern, the people commanded her to go up on to it; which she did, first making the sign of the cross.

15) Then the people set fire to the pile. Though the flame was incredibly large, it did not touch her, for God took compassion on her, and caused a great eruption from the earth beneath, and a cloud from above to pour down great quantities of rain and hail;

16) Insomuch that by the rupture of the earth, very many were in great danger, and some were killed, the fire was extinguished, and Thecla was preserved.

Chapter VI

1) In the mean time Paul, together with Onesiphorus, his wife and children, was keeping a fast in a certain cave, which was in the road from Iconium to Daphne.

Some interpretations of the text give the idea that Paul surreptitiously fled the area and left Thecla to suffer and die alone. The viewpoint of these scholars seems to be that it was a more cowardly act to retreat to a cave away from the city and pray for Thecla from a distance than it would have been to make his way back into the city to somehow defend or comfort Thecla during her trials or death. The text indicates that Paul was taken outside the city to be whipped. It is likely he was escorted out of the city, beaten, and told not to come back into the city since he and Thecla had caused such a disturbance. Whether he lost his courage and left instead of trying to go back in and risk his life is up to the reader to ponder.

2) And when they had fasted for several days, the children said to Paul, "Father, we are hungry, and have not wherewithal to buy bread;" for

Onesiphorus, with his family, had left all his money and possessions to follow Paul.

3) Then Paul, taking off his coat, said to the boy, "Go, child, and buy bread, and bring it back here."

4) But while the boy was buying the bread, he saw his neighbor, Thecla and he was surprised. He said to her, "Thecla, where are you going?"

5) She replied, "I am in pursuit of Paul, having been delivered from the flames."

6) The boy then said, "I will bring you to him, for he is greatly concern about you, and has been in prayer and fasting the last six days."

7) When Thecla came to the cave, she found Paul upon his knees praying and saying, "O holy Father, O Lord Jesus Christ, grant that the fire may not touch Thecla. Be her helper, for she is your servant."

8) Thecla, was standing behind him and cried out and said: "O sovereign Lord, Creator of heaven and earth, the Father of your beloved and holy Son, I praise you that you have preserved me from the fire, to see Paul again."

9) Then Paul arose, and when he saw her, said, "O God, who examines the heart, Father of my Lord Jesus Christ, I praise you because you have answered my prayer."

10) And there prevailed among them in the cave an entire affection to each other; Paul, Onesiphorus, and all that were with them being filled with joy.

11) They had five loaves, some herbs, and water, and they took solace with each other and reflected upon the holy works of Christ.

12) Then Thecla said to Paul, "If you are pleased with it, I will follow you where ever you go."

13) He replied to her, "People are more likely to want to have sex these days, and you being so beautiful, I am afraid that you may meet with greater temptation than in times before, and I worry that you may not stand against the temptation, but be overcome by it."

14) Thecla replied, "Grant me only the seal of Christ, and no temptation shall affect me."

15) Paul answered, "Thecla, wait with patience, and you shall receive the gift of Christ."

Chapter VII

1) Then Paul sent Onesiphorus and his family back to their own home, and he took Thecla along with him and they went to Antioch;

2) And as soon as they came into the city, a certain Syrian, named Alexander, a magistrate, in the city, who had done many considerable services for the city during his magistracy saw Thecla and fell in love with her. He endeavored by giving Paul many expensive gifts to bribe Paul to act in his interest.

3) But Paul told him, "I know not the woman of whom you speak, nor does she belong to me."

Like Abraham told the foreign king a "half-lie" about Sarah in order to avoid conflict, Paul lies to the man about Thecla. Neither event ended well.

NASB - Genesis 20:1 Now Abraham journeyed from there toward the land of the Negev, and settled between Kadesh and Shur; then he sojourned in Gerar. 2Abraham said of Sarah his wife, "She is my sister." So Abimelech king of Gerar sent and took Sarah. 3But God came to Abimelech in a dream of the night, and said to him, "Behold, you are a dead man because of the woman whom you have taken, for she is married."...

4) But he, being a person of great power in Antioch, seized her in the street and kissed her; which Thecla would not tolerate, but looking around for Paul, she cried out in a distressed loud tone, "Do not force me. I do not know you. I am a stranger. Do not force me. I am a servant of God; I am one of the principal persons of Iconium, and was obliged to leave that city because I would not be married to Thamyris."

5) Then she laid hold on Alexander, tore his coat, and took his crown off his head, and made him appear ridiculous before all the people.

6) But Alexander, partly as he loved her, and partly being ashamed of what had been done, led her to the governor. When Thecla confessed about what she had done, the governor condemned her to be thrown among the beasts.

Chapter VIII

1) But when the people saw what her punishment

was they said: "The judgments passed in this city are unjust. But Thecla begged the favor of the governor and asked that her chastity might not be attacked, but preserved till she should be cast to the beasts."

Thecla knew that if left in prison the guards and prisoners would have their way with her and she would die in a defiled state, being raped and abused."

2) The governor then asked, "Who would give her a place to stay?" Upon which a certain very rich widow, named Trifina, whose daughter was lately dead, desired that she might have the keeping of her; and she began to treat her in her house as her own daughter.

3) In time the day came when the beasts were to be brought out to be seen (by the people of the city); and Thecla was brought to the amphitheatre, and put into a den with a very fierce lioness in the presence of a multitude of spectators.

4) Trifina, without any hesitation, accompanied

Thecla. And the lioness licked the feet of Thecla. The title written which denotes her crime was: "Sacrilege." Then the woman cried out, "O God, the judgments of this city are unrighteous."

5) After the beasts had been shown, Trifina took Thecla home with her, and they went to bed; and behold, the daughter of Trifina, who was dead, appeared to her mother, and said, "Mother, let the young woman, Thecla, be proclaimed by you as your daughter in my place. Ask her to pray for me, that I may be translated to a state of happiness."

The word, "translated" is used to describe a change of a state of being, physically and/or spiritually. It is much like the word used when Jesus was on the mount of Transfiguration where he and his clothing began to shine like the sun.

Matthew 17 Holman Christian Standard Bible (HCSB)
17 After six days Jesus took Peter, James, and his brother John and led them up on a high mountain by themselves. 2 He was transformed [a] in front of them, and His face shone like the sun. Even His clothes became as white as

the light. 3 Suddenly, Moses and Elijah appeared to them, talking with Him.

It should be noted that Jews at this time did not have the same concept of heaven as that which became part of the Christian belief. In or around the fourth century C.E. Jews began to speculate about an afterlife. Traditional Judaism firmly believes that death is not the end of human existence. However, Judaism is primarily focused on life here and now rather than on the afterlife. Judaism does not have much dogma about the afterlife, and leaves a great deal of room for personal opinion. It is possible for an Orthodox Jew to believe that the souls of the righteous dead go to a place similar to the Christian heaven, or that they are reincarnated through many lifetimes, or that they simply wait until the coming of the messiah, when they will be resurrected. Likewise, Orthodox Jews can believe that the souls of the wicked are tormented by demons of their own creation, or that wicked souls are simply destroyed at death, ceasing to exist.

Some scholars claim that belief in the afterlife is a

teaching that developed late in Jewish history. It is true that the Torah emphasizes immediate, concrete, physical rewards and punishments rather than abstract future ones. However, there is clear evidence in the Torah of belief in existence after death. The Torah speaks of several noteworthy people being "gathered to their people."

The New Testament speaks of a great divide between those in torment and those who are "in the bosom of Abraham." This parable was spoken by Jesus prior to his death and sacrifice and is thus considered an Old Testament teaching.

Luke 16: 19 "There was a rich man who would dress in purple and fine linen, feasting lavishly every day. 20 But a poor man named Lazarus, covered with sores, was left at his gate. 21 He longed to be filled with what fell from the rich man's table, but instead the dogs would come and lick his sores. 22 One day the poor man died and was carried away by the angels to Abraham's side. The rich man also died and was buried. 23 And being in torment in Hades, he looked up and saw Abraham a long way off, with Lazarus at his side. 24 'Father Abraham!' he called out, 'Have mercy on me and send Lazarus to dip the tip of his finger in water and cool my tongue, because I am in agony in this flame!'

25 "'Son,' Abraham said, 'remember that during your life you received your good things, just as Lazarus received bad things, but now he is comforted here, while you are in agony. 26 Besides all this, a great chasm has been fixed between us and you, so that those who want to pass over from here to you cannot; neither can those from there cross over to us.'

27 "'Father,' he said, 'then I beg you to send him to my father's house — 28 because I have five brothers — to warn them, so they won't also come to this place of torment.'

29 "But Abraham said, 'they have Moses and the prophets; they should listen to them.'

30 "'No, father Abraham,' he said. 'But if someone from the dead goes to them, they will repent.'

31 "But he told him, 'If they don't listen to Moses and the prophets, they will not be persuaded if someone rises from the dead.'"

For Trifina's daughter to request prayers for "translation" to a place of happiness may be a reference to the words spoken by Jesus that he would go and prepare a place for those who believe in him. Falconilla may be asking to be translated to that place of joy.

6) Upon which Trifina, with a mournful air, said, "My daughter Falconilla has appeared to me, and ordered me to receive you in her room. I desire you to pray for my daughter, that she may be translated into a state of happiness, and to life eternal."

7) When Thecla heard this, she immediately prayed to the Lord, and said, "O Lord God of heaven and earth, Jesus Christ, You are the Son of the Most High. Grant that her daughter, Falconilla may live forever."   Trifina hearing this groaned again, and said, "O unrighteous judgments! O unreasonable wickedness! that such a creature should (again) be cast to the beasts!"

8) The next day, at break of day, Alexander came to Trifina's house, and said, "The governor and the people are waiting; bring the criminal out."

9) But Trifina attacked him so violently that he was

frightened, and ran away. Trifina was a member of the royal family; and she thus expressed her sorrow, and said, "Alas, I have trouble in my house on two accounts, and there is no one who will relieve me, either from the loss of my daughter, or my being able to save Thecla. But now, O Lord God, be the helper of Thecla your servant."

10) While she was engaged in prayer, the governor sent one of his own officers to bring Thecla. Trifina took her by the hand, and went with her. Trifina said, "I went with Falconilla to her grave, and now must go with Thecla to the beasts."

11) When Thecla heard this, she wept and prayed, and said, "O Lord God, whom I have made my confidence and refuge, reward Trifina for her compassion to me, and preserving my chastity."

12) Upon this there was a great noise in the amphitheatre; the beasts roared, and the people cried out, "Bring in the criminal."

13) But the woman cried out, and said, "Let the whole city suffer for such crimes; and order all of

us, O governor, to the same punishment. O unjust judgment! O cruel sight!"

14) Others said, "Let the whole city be destroyed for this vile action. Kill us all, O governor. O cruel sight! O unrighteous judgment."

Chapter IX

1) Then Thecla was taken out of the hand of Trifina, stripped naked, had a girdle put on, and thrown into the place appointed for fighting with the beasts: and the lions and the bears were let loose upon her.

The girdle, in this case, was likely a wide piece of cloth worn around the hips.

2) But a lioness, which was the fiercest of all, ran to Thecla, and fell down at her feet. Upon which the multitude of women shouted aloud.

3) Then a female bear ran fiercely towards her; but the lioness intercepted the bear, and tore it to pieces.

4) Again, a lion, which was know to devour men, and which belonged to Alexander, ran towards her; but the lioness challenged the lion, and they killed each other.

5) The women were worried and anxious because the lioness, which had helped Thecla, was dead.

6) Afterwards, they brought out many other wild beasts; but Thecla stood with her hands stretched towards heaven, and prayed; and when she had done praying, she turned about, and saw a pit of water, and said, "Now it is a proper time for me to be baptized."

7) Accordingly she threw herself into the water, and said, "In thy name, O my Lord Jesus Christ, I am this last day baptized." The women and the people seeing this, cried out, and said, "Do not throw yourself into the water." And the governor himself cried out, to think that the fish (sea-calves) were like to devour so much beauty.

8) Notwithstanding all this, Thecla threw herself into the water, in the name of our Lord Jesus Christ.

9) But the fish (sea-calves,) when they saw the lighting and fire, were killed, and swam dead upon the surface of the water, and a cloud of fire surrounded Thecla, so that as the beasts could not come near her, so the people could not see her nakedness.

In modern terms, the only animal well known as a sea calf is a harbor seal. Some of the older commentaries refer to the calf as a seal. This creature, called a sea calf, had to be large enough to kill a human. It was placed in the pit to kill anyone who ventured in. The creature had to be carnivorous, aggressive, and small enough for several to fit and survive in a pit in the midst of an amphitheater filled with water. This "fish" or "sea calf" may be a seal or it could be a crocodile. Today, no crocodiles survive in Turkey but in the day of the writing of The Acts of Paul and Thecla the Nile crocodile was found in the area.

10) Then they turned other wild beasts upon her but they made a very mournful outcry; and from the crowd came out a mist of spikenard, and cassia,

and amomus [a sort of spikenard, or the herb of Jerusalem, or ladies-rose], and from the crowd came ointment; so much that the quantity of ointment was large, in proportion to the number of people. Then all the beasts lay down as if they had fallen fast asleep, and they did not touch Thecla.

Why people in the crowd had spikenard, cassia, and ointment with them we are not told. The effect of the herbs, spikenard and ointment was to sedate the beasts.

11) Whereupon Alexander said to the Governor, "I have some very fierce and aggressive bulls; let us tie her to them." To which the governor, with concern, replied, "You may do what you think fit."

12) Then they put a cord round Thecla's waist, which bound also her feet, and with it tied her to the bulls, to whose genitals they applied red-hot irons, that so they being the more tormented, might more violently drag Thecla about, till they had killed her.

13) The bulls accordingly tore about, making a

most hideous noise, but the flame, which was about Thecla, burnt off the cords, which were fastened to the members of the bulls, and she stood in the middle of the stage, as unconcerned as if she had not been bound.

14) But in the mean time, Trifina, who sat upon one of the benches, fainted away and died; upon which the whole city became very anxious and fearful.

15) And Alexander himself was afraid, and desired the governor, saying, "I beg you to take compassion on me and the city, and release this woman, who has fought with the beasts or both you and I will be killed by the whole city."

16) "For if Caesar should have any account of what has passed now, he will certainly immediately destroy the city, because Trifina, a person of royal linage, and a relation of his, is dead upon her seat."

17) Upon this the governor called Thecla from among the beasts to him, and said to her, "Who are you? Why is it that not one of the beasts will touch you?"

18) Thecla replied to him, "I am a servant of the living God; and as to my state, I am a believer of

Jesus Christ his Son, in whom God is well pleased; and for that reason none of the beasts could touch me.

19) He alone is the way to eternal salvation, and the foundation of eternal life. He is a refuge to those who are in distress; a support to the afflicted, hope and defense to those who are hopeless; and, in a word, all those who do not believe on him, shall not live, but suffer eternal death."

20) When the governor heard these things, he ordered her clothes to be brought, and said to her, "Put on your clothes."

21) Thecla replied, "May that God who clothed me when I was naked among the beasts, in the Day of Judgment clothe your soul with the robe of salvation. Then she took her clothes, and put them on; and the governor immediately published an order in these words, "I release to you Thecla, the servant of God."

22) Upon which the women cried out together with a loud voice, and with one accord gave praise to God, and said, "There is but one God, who is the

God of Thecla; the one God who hath delivered Thecla."

23) So loud were their voices that the whole city seemed to be shaken; and Trifina herself heard the glad tidings, and arose again, and ran with the multitude to meet Thecla; and embracing her said, "Now I believe there shall be a resurrection of the dead; now I am persuaded that my daughter is alive. Come home with me, my daughter Thecla, and I will bequeath all that I have to you."

24) So Thecla went with Trifina, and was entertained there a few days, teaching her the word of the Lord, whereby many young women were converted; and there was great joy in the family of Trifina.

25) But Thecla longed to see Paul, and inquired and sent everywhere to find him and when after a time she was informed that he was at Myra, in Lycia, she took with her many young men and women; and putting on a girdle (wide belt), and dressing herself in the fashion of a man, she went to him in Myra in Lycia, and there found Paul preaching the word of God; and she stood by him

among the crowd.

Lycia (Greek: Λυκία, Turkish: Likya) was a geopolitical region in Anatolia in what are now the provinces of Antalya and Muğla on the southern coast of Turkey, and Burdur Province inland. Myra is an ancient town in Lycia where the small town of Kale (Demre) is situated today in present day Antalya Province of Turkey. It was located on the river Myros, in the fertile alluvial plain between Alaca Dağ, the Massikytos range and the Aegean Sea.

Chapter X

1) Paul was very surprised when he saw her and the people with her and he imagined some new trial was going to besiege them.

Paul realized that wherever Thecla went trouble was bound to follow.

2) Which when Thecla realized what Paul was thinking, she said to him, "I have been baptized,

Paul. He who assists you in preaching has assisted me to baptize."

3) Then Paul took her, and led her to the house of Hermes; and Thecla related to Paul all that had befallen her in Antioch. And Paul was amazed, and all who heard were confirmed in the faith, and prayed for Trifina's happiness.

4) Then Thecla arose, and said to Paul, I am going to Iconium. Paul replied to her, "Go, and teach the word of the Lord."

5) But Trifina had sent large sums of money to Paul, and also clothing by the hands of Thecla, for the relief of the poor.

6) So Thecla went to Iconium. And when she came to the house of Onesiphorus, she fell down upon the floor where Paul had sat and preached, and mixing her tears with her prayers, she praised and glorified God in the following words:

17) "O Lord, the God of this house in which I was first enlightened by you; O Jesus, son of the living God, who was my helper before the governor, my helper in the fire, and my helper among the beasts; you alone are God forever and ever. Amen."

8) When Thecla returned she found Thamyris dead, but her mother living. So calling her mother, she said to her, "Theoclia, my mother, is it possible for you to be brought to a belief, that there is but one Lord God, who dwells in the heavens? If you desire great riches, God will give them to you by me; if you want (to see) your daughter again, I am here."

9) These and many other things she testified to her mother, as she endeavored to persuade her mother. But her mother Theoclia gave no credit to the things, which were said by the martyr Thecla.

It is more difficult for family and friends to take the convert seriously. The past clouds judgment and a prophet is not respected in his own land.

10) When Thecla realized her words were of no purpose (made no difference), she made the sign of the cross over her whole body and she left the house and went to Daphine. When she came there, she went to the cave, where she had found Paul

with Onesiphorus, and fell down on the ground; and wept before God.

11) When she departed from there she went to Seleucia, and enlightened many in the knowledge of Christ.

12) And a bright cloud went with her in her journey.

13) And after she had arrived at Seleucia, she went to a place out of the city, about the distance of a furlong, being afraid of the inhabitants, because they were worshippers of idols.

A furlong is about one-eighth of a mile, equivalent to 660 feet, 220 yards.

14) And the cloud led her into a mountain called Calamon, or Rodeon. There she lived for many years, and underwent a great many vexing temptations of the devil, which she endured gracefully by the assistance which she had from Christ.

15) After a long time certain wealthy women heard about the virgin Thecla and went to visit her.

Thecla instructed them in the oracles of God, and many of them abandoned this world, and led a monastic life with her.

16) Because of this a good report was spread everywhere of Thecla, and she worked several miraculous cures, so that all the city and surrounding countries brought their sick to that mountain, and before they came as far as the door of the cave, they were instantly cured of whatsoever disease they had.

17) The unclean spirits were cast out, making a noise. All received their sick cured, and they all glorified God, who had bestowed such power on the virgin Thecla;

18) Because of her cures the physicians of Seleucia were no longer needed, and they lost all the profit of their trade, because no one paid attention to them. So because of this they were filled with envy and began to plan a method to dispatch this servant of Christ.

Chapter XI

1) The devil then suggested evil advice to their minds and so on a certain day they met together to plan. They reasoned among themselves thinking, "The virgin is a priestess of the great goddess Diana, and whatsoever she requests from her, is granted, because she is a virgin, and so is beloved by all the gods.

2) Now then let us use some brutish fellows, and after we have made them sufficiently drunk, and given them a good sum of money, let us order them to go and rape this virgin. We will promise them that if they do it we will give them a larger reward."

3) (For they thus concluded among themselves, that if they be able to spoil (rape) her, the gods will no more listen to her, nor Diana cure the sick for her.)

The physicians were not aware of the new religion of Christianity or if they had heard of it they did not connect Thecla to this new sect. Instead, they assumed Thecla belonged to the religions with which they were familiar. They new that the miracles Thecla performed left them few if any sick people to treat and thus little to no income.

4) They proceeded according to their plans, and the brutish men went to the mountain, and attacked the cave in which Thecla was dwelling. And they were as fierce as lions, knocking at the door.

5) The holy martyr Thecla, relied upon the God in whom she believed. Even though she had been warned of their plan she opened the door and said to them, "Young men, what is your business?"

6) They replied, "Is there any one within, whose name is Thecla?" She answered, "Why are you looking for her?" They said, "We want to have sex with her."

7) The blessed Thecla answered, "Though I am a mean old woman, I am the servant of my Lord Jesus Christ; and though you have a vile design against me, you shall not be able to accomplish it." They replied, "It is impossible for you to fight us off. We will be able to do with you what we have a mind."

8) And while they were saying this, they grabbed

her with force to ravish her. Then she with gentleness and mildness said to them, "Young men have patience, and see the glory of the Lord."

9) And while they held her, she looked up to heaven and said, "O God, most reverend to whom none can be likened; who make yourself glorious over your enemies. You delivered me from the fire, and did not give me up to Thamyris. You did not give me up to Alexander. You delivered me from the wild beasts. You preserved me in the deep waters. You have always been my helper, and have glorified your name in me.

10) Now also, deliver me from the hands of these wicked and unreasonable men. Do not allow them to rape me for I have up to this time preserved my honor for you. I love you and long for you, and worship you, O Father, Son, and Holy Ghost, for evermore. Amen."

11) Then there came a voice from heaven saying, "Fear not, Thecla, my faithful servant, for I am with you. Look and see the place, which is opened for you. There is where your eternal abode shall be; there you shall receive a beautiful vision."

12) Then the blessed Thecla looked and she saw the rock opened with a large gap so that a man might enter in. Then she did as God commanded her and bravely fled from the vile group, and went into the rock, which instantly closed so tightly that there was not even a crack that was visible where it had been opened.

13) The men froze in place, completely astonished at such a great miracle, and they had no power to detain the servant of God. But they were only able to catch hold of her veil, or hood and they tore off a piece of it.

14) And even that was by the permission of God, for the confirmation of their faith for those who should come to see this venerable place, and to convey blessings to those in succeeding ages, who should believe on our Lord Jesus Christ from a pure heart.

15) This is how the great martyr, virgin, and apostle of God, Thecla came from Iconium at eighteen years of age and afterwards journeyed and traveled, and lived a monastic life in the cave

where she lived seventy-two years, so that she was
ninety years old when the Lord translated her.

*The text calls Thecla an apostle. She was translated
(taken up to heave) like Enoch. These two statements
leave the ancient reader with the strong indication that
Thecla was of the same spiritual status as Paul and was
as loved by God as Enoch.*

16) Thus ends her life.

17) The day, which is kept sacred to her memory, is
the twenty-fourth of September, to the glory of the
Father, and the Son, and the Holy Ghost, now and
for evermore. Amen.

Joseph Lumpkin